Letters to Anna

by
Cathy Pfeil

Balboa Press books may be ordered through booksellers or by contacting:

Balboa Press
A Division of Hay House
1663 Liberty Drive
Bloomington, IN 47403
www.balboapress.com
1-(877) 407-4847

Because of the dynamic nature of the Internet, any web addresses or links contained in this book may have changed since publication and may no longer be valid. The views expressed in this work are solely those of the author and do not necessarily reflect the views of the publisher, and the publisher hereby disclaims any responsibility for them.

The author of this book does not dispense medical advice or prescribe the use of any technique as a form of treatment for physical, emotional, or medical problems without the advice of a physician, either directly or indirectly. The intent of the author is only to offer information of a general nature to help you in your quest for emotional and spiritual well-being. In the event you use any of the information in this book for yourself, which is your constitutional right, the author and the publisher assume no responsibility for your actions.

Any people depicted in stock imagery provided by Thinkstock are models, and such images are being used for illustrative purposes only.
Certain stock imagery © Thinkstock.

Printed in the United States of America

ISBN: 978-1-4525-6721-1 (sc)
ISBN: 978-1-4525-6722-8 (e)

Balboa Press rev. date: 1/17/2013

BALBOA.
PRESS
A DIVISION OF HAY HOUSE

To all the Children in my life

Acknowledgments

I want to thank my family for allowing me the time and energy to always follow my path. I am in blessed thanksgiving to my husband, Chuck, and my Sarah and Heather, and their beautiful families.

I am so grateful that my friend and apprentice Anna is in my life. I am grateful for her questioning mind and her amazing vision.

I am grateful for those who have supported my writing--Frances Tibbits, Dolly Mae and especially my wonderful partner of 40 years, Chuck Pfeil. Thank you to Rev. Charles Hall; all the Practitioners at Genesis Global Spiritual Center in Burien, Washington; and my Dean, the teachers, and my fellow students in the Holmes Institute of Consciousness Studies.

To the next generation of shiny children, the world is filled with gatekeepers to show you the way. And finally I give great thanks to my especially shiny new apprentices and grandchildren, Alexandra Rose, Oliver Charles and Nora Marjorie.

Table of Contents

One

We are members of a vast cosmic orchestra

For Anna:

> *"We are members of a vast cosmic orchestra*
> *in which each living instrument is essential*
> *to the complementary*
> *and harmonious playing of the whole."*
> *Kinship of all Life* by J.Allen Boone

I have known Anna since she was five years old. Her family had moved to our town with the expectation that Anna would attend the local Waldorf School. A beautiful and vivacious child, Anna started asking me questions the first time we met. Over the years my husband, Chuck, and I have become dear friends with her family, but it has always been my relationship with the unique and amazing Anna that has cemented our relationship. She is in every sense of the word my apprentice.

I had moved to Olympia with my family many years before I met Anna to help start the very Waldorf School that Anna enrolled in. As a Waldorf Kindergarten teacher I was taught to honor those sleepy children who had never watched television, never played with plastic toys or been exposed to computers. Anna came in awake and aware. Needless to say, this particular school was not the school for her.

Needing no outside stimulation to create the desire to know more, Anna came in with an insatiable curiosity that both served and separated her from many of her peers. Anna needs to know why. She sees and grieves for what is not fair in the world and has little time for adults who misrepresent themselves, teachers teaching on autopilot and has little time for the social trappings of being a teenager. Most of all Anna has always known she is destined to make a difference in the world and that she will.

Brilliantly Anna has surrounded herself with a whole group of adults who see her and know who she is. Besides being born to an off-the-scale intelligent mother and father, Anna has collected adults in many area of expertise to assist her to uncover the secrets of the universe.

For her Bat Mitzvah I gave her a copy of all my writings up until that point, including parts of a book I had been working on, a kind of rite-of-passage into a deeper level of her apprenticeship with me, and a moment when it came together for me that I was a teacher of this generation.

Over the years I created jobs that allowed me to have plenty of time with my own children who also fit the profile of what is called Indigo children. I assisted a midwife and taught childbirth classes through the 70's, taught preschool and kindergarten through the 80's then began teaching metaphysics in the early 90's after a spiritual awakening. I consider myself a gatekeeper. I make the path just a bit smoother. I assisted in gentle births, offered a comforting teaching environment then began to answer their questions. I let them know that they are not alone, that they are here on purpose by divine appointment and we welcome them wholly.

There are various books out here about the "new children" coming onto the planet. Whatever you call it, the trend towards these gifted children is very real. Because my belief is simply "All is One" and "All is Now" the children being identified now as Indigo and Crystal are not a separate group of beings arriving, but aspects of ourselves in an unfolding and maturing consciousness.

I am not focusing on the concept of Indigos and Crystals in this book and would highly recommend starting with "The Indigo Children: The New Kids Have Arrived" by Jan Tober and Lee Carroll.

REPORTED CHARACTERISTICS OF AN INDIGO CHILD

Various authors/therapists have given their opinions. Below are some of the characteristics cited for Indigo children:

- Come into the world with a feeling of royalty (and often act like it).
- Have a feeling of "deserving to be here", and are surprised when others don't share that.
- Do not have an issue with self-worth. They often tell the parents "who they are."
- Have difficulty with absolute authority (authority without explanation or choice).
- Simply will not do certain things; for example, waiting in line is difficult for them.
- Get frustrated with systems that are ritually oriented and don't require creative thought.
- Often see better ways of doing things, both at home and in school, which makes them seem like "system busters" (nonconforming to any system).
- Seem anti-social unless they are with their own kind. If there are no others of like consciousness around them, they often turn inward; feeling like no other human understands them. School is often extremely difficult for them socially.
- Will not respond to "guilt" discipline ("Wait till your father gets home and finds out what you did").
- Are not shy in letting you know what they need.

(Excerpt from *The Indigo Children: The New Kids Have Arrived* by Jan Tober and Lee Carroll)

My husband Chuck met Anna before I did. He went to meet our new neighbors soon after their arrival and Anna fell instantly in love with him, calling him Chuck-a-file. She was wary of me, because I was married to her Chuck-a-file, and a roadblock to her plan to marry him.

When Anna and I met she was surrounded by a huge glowing light. Gleaming with bright dark eyes and a wonderful smile, Anna was unnerving at five years old with her direct manner and a high level of clarity. This was not your average five-year-old by a long shot. Whatever Anna was thinking she tended to simply say, and Anna was thinking of many things. Of course this got her in trouble many times as she learned to navigate social norms.

One time I was preparing for guests and Anna was asking me questions about who was coming and by the time they arrived she was ready with a long list of somewhat personal questions she needed answered immediately. "Hello, nice to meet you, Cathy says you are trying to have a baby. How is that going?" Yikes. Her curiosity simply overwhelmed all social constructs. Good for her, she is her genuine authentic self. From the very beginning we clicked. She gave up her plan of marrying Chuck and she and I became fast friends.

It was as if Anna and I were fulfilling some grand divine appointment in this lifetime.

In grace and ease, Cathy

Two

How you think about things pictures out into reality

My Dear Anna:

Here you are at the end of your high school experience. Thank you so much for including us in your graduation evening. I thought I would write a few things that I want to make sure you got one way or another while staying with us this year.

First and most important is that how you think about things out picture into reality. Everything manifests. Watch your negative thoughts because when you hold anger or negative opinions they will create themselves. This goes for everyone and every situation. You have to be ninja-smart sometimes to stay ahead of manifesting negatively, and I know you are or I would not have made you my apprentice all those years ago.

Top on the list of whom you tend to create negative thoughts about is you. When you think negatively about yourself you can manifest that negative reality in a snap.

Spend time, even a short time like 10 minutes, in meditation every day.

Talk regularly to someone who thinks positively and can act as your mentor to help you maintain positive thinking.

Start ditching friends who think and act negatively, even if they have been your friend since third grade. Surround yourself only with positive, like-minded people.

Before you go to sleep at night write down a couple good things that happened in your day.

Always remember that you are a reflection of your thoughts.

Love,
Cathy

Three

I have so much to ask you!

Dear Cathy:

I wanted first of all to thank you for making me your apprentice. I've read different parts of your book that you gave me of your experiences at different times before. I've tried, but there were things I did not always understand. It frustrates me because though I've learned and experienced a lot of things this year (I probably can understand your book maybe a little bit better now) however, there are still things that fascinate me. I want to know so much. I have so much that I have to ask you. That is why I am putting them in this book because I do not have time to ask you everything at once. At least you can answer if you want to answer my questions at all, on paper. Or when you have the time and energy to, whenever you want to. I hope this project makes you think. I hope also that you enjoy this project. Thanks for being my friend and teacher.

With love and good energy and excited curiosity…

Anna

Four

So we come in groups?

Dear Cathy,

So … we come in groups? Spiritual groups on earth and afterwards? Why? When are we supposed to be alone? When together? Why are we born alone? Why do we die alone? How does our death and birth connect to these groups?

Love,

Anna

Well Anna, you are starting with a bang!

Yes, I do believe we come in groups. One way of thinking about this is that before we are born a whole group of spiritual beings who all love us very much sit down at a big table to hear about what you want to learn about in this lifetime. Say you want to learn about loving relationships. So these spirits decide what role they are going to play out for you to get the best and most exciting class in loving relationships. And the class will take your whole life. And some of the roles these spirits will play are very hard and sometimes hurtful.

It's like they say, Anna, I love you so much and support you in learning about loving relationships that I will play the role of a friend who loves you, then I will leave and hurt you. Why? Well, learning something doesn't mean you just learn the good stuff. To really understand something you have to explore it 360 degrees. With the Loving Relationship class you unfortunately need to know what not loving feels like to really love.

Oh, and I forgot to say that once you come to earth you forget what classes you signed up for. Rats. It would be so much easier if we retained that information!

So do I think there is actually a pre-birth conference? Of course not. It is just a way of explaining that every situation has its own inherent opportunity for you to grow and learn. You are always in choice. If you want to receive an "A+" in "life-school" and take a step back and look at the big picture you can; or you can flounder in the "C" range and go on thinking that bad things just seem to happen for no reason. If you choose the bad things happen route, they certainly will occur, because it is your creation!

So next question: Are we in spiritual groups on earth and afterwards? Of course! One answer is that we need these other spirits around us, other aspects of the Divine Nature that we all are to reflect off of. Another answer is what seems like a bunch of separate beings are all actually aspects of the same thing. In that way we are never alone, not when we are born, not when we die.

The aspect that feels alone, the observer self, always analyzes the situation from an individual perspective. Problem solving, looking at the details and making decisions are part of that self. Sometimes we confuse our "little self" as the whole enchilada rather than just one aspect of our consciousness. We have lonely experiences for sure; we can also expand our thinking out to the bigger field of consciousness and see beyond our limited thinking.

So, in a nut shell; we are part of one huge consciousness. Within that consciousness we are constantly growing and learning about ourselves and our connection to spirit.

In grace and ease,

Cathy

Five

Name Game

Cathy,

    I have heard you talk about the power in people's names. I know some people change their names. Are they changing it to their true name? How do we know our true name and how does a name hold power?

Anna

Anna:

> *Our birth is but a sleep and a forgetting:*
> *The Soul that rises with us, our life's Star,*
> *Hath had elsewhere its setting,*
> *And cometh from afar:*
> *Not in entire forgetfulness,*
> *And not in utter nakedness,*
> *But trailing clouds of glory do we come*
> *From God, who is our home:*
> *Heaven lies about us in our infancy!*

By William Wordsworth from *Ode. Intimations of Immortality*

I love this poem by Wordsworth. "Trailing clouds of glory" we bring with us innate information and connection to the Divine right into our human experience. Babies totally trust. It is our sacred responsibility as the adults who surround babies to nurture this amazing connection and keep that connection to the Divine. Keeping children in touch with their "life's star" is crucial to maintaining that connection. So how do we do that? Hopefully the parents are listening closely to those trails of glory and resonate with the vibrations they bring through into this world. The sound of our name should bring a certain resonance that just fits with that child. Susie? Jane? Should we name her after Aunt Gertrude? Whatever the ultimate choice parents choose the name that resonates to that child.

My friend Dolly Mae has written a wonderful book about names and how to understand what your name holds energetically. Dolly explains names as energy packets based on the letters and the arrangement of these letters. I only know a small bit in comparison to Dolly. Be sure to ask her about your name. This is what I know about your name, Anna:

A First letter notes that you are independent, self-aware and focused.

NN You need change and variety. Double constants mean obsessive, compulsive behavior. So it could be an obsessive, compulsive need for change and variety!

A Last letter shows you will up-level in this lifetime, emotionally, mentally and spiritually. Fast work makes it feel as if you are having many lifetimes in one. Strong empathy.

(Excerpt from *If You Have a Name You Need This Book* by Dolly Mae)

Do I believe this is true that every person is named at birth with a name that resonates to their soul level? No. Sometimes people change their names to one that just sounds better to them. Some aspect they are focusing on. I do not suggest changing your name. I know a woman who changed her name every time she felt "spirit led."

Usually her name change would happen while driving on the freeway. Go figure. I never knew what to call her, Fern, Crystal, Angel… I would just start naming all her names at once, Fern-Crystal-Angel, whatever! Don't go there!

Hopefully your name will resonate clearly for you and you can use it as a touch stone as you enter an often materialistic and cynical world that needs a little bit more "Anna" who is independent, self-aware and focused; with an obsessive-compulsive need for change and variety; who is up-leveling emotionally, mentally and spiritually; with strong empathy.

In grace,
Cathy

Six

Psychic & powerful indigo child

Cathy,

How can you tell if someone is psychic-powerful--an indigo child? What are the types and differences?

Anna

My dear Anna:

I want to start with the main idea you will hear me say a zillion times--All Is One. Every question you ask is always going to have this truth as the starting point.

Every person without exception is an aspect of that Divine Nature. We manifest that connection and act in ways that fulfill our divine connected self in many different ways. As we become more aware of our connection and fill out into that connection more clearly it cannot help but show.

When we are also manifesting our connection, by being aware and living this principle, we can see it in others.

The actual answer to how you can tell if someone is "gifted" or imbued with this creative Yes energy is to be connected yourself. The more you practice seeing the Divine in everyone and every situation the more powerful people you will see emerge in your landscape.

Let's talk about psychics first. In connecting to the Divine Source you are always going to get back what you put into it. When someone asks a question that is on a physical level like, "Is Harry the right man for me?" or "Will I win the Lotto?" The answer will meet the level of the questioner, no matter how in tune the reader is. You order a hot dog, you get a hot dog.

To actually sit with someone who is spiritually connected and together move into the flow can be a deep and rich experience. This usually, although not always, takes your attention and focus and is not something you run into at a mini-session at a psychic fair.

Also the level from which someone is getting their information can influence the answer as well as the question. I believe you can use anything as a gateway into Divine Consciousness. A set of cards, a crystal on a string or looking at the stars all can have validity to the level the participants are connected to Source. But I also believe these tools; though helpful for beginners, begin to limit the level of access one can have.

An indigo child refers to the children and now young adults who are on the planet after the last major planetary energy shift. Like I talked about before when we discussed if we choose to be born, we are attached to the energies that will assist us to know ourselves and our connection to the One more clearly.

There are waves of energy up leveling on the planet. We have gone through a major shift recently that is beginning to draw more energy that resonates with the new level of vibration here on earth. These people with this new vibration have not come all at once, but began trickling through in the last age and have increased dramatically now.

Powerful People – hmmm…

Power happens on many levels--having control is powerful, having money is powerful, and being in charge is very powerful. Even being tricky can be powerful. Real power lies in…okay, fill in the blank here Anna… _____.

If you wrote that true power always is from our connection to ourselves and through our connection to the One you are correct!

But your question is how would you be able to tell? Here are a couple clues, feel free to continue the list…

Real power lies in…inner stillness

Real power lies in…joy

Real power lies in…love

Real power lies in…simply listening

Real power lies in… the flow

Real power lies in…acting out of compassion

Much love and support to you
on your journey into knowing,

Cathy

Seven

Why do we need to give?

Dear Cathy,

Thank you for being my Cathy! You are so positive and I am so happy to have you in my life. Why do we need to give? Why is it important? Is it because we need to exchange energy to form bonds?

I love you so much!

Always,
Anna

Dear Anna:

You are getting it! Yes, that is correct. So now use my hypothesis of All is One to double check why this would be so. When you give, whom are you actually giving to?

The act of giving freely is like releasing yourself to the flow of the One. This release creates an opportunity for receiving. Giving freely means you are not attached to what is on the receiver's side. If you are thinking, "I will get this if I give that" this is not in the flow. Think instead "I release this money, item, time or even an idea, freely".

The act of tithing, giving a percentage of your income to what supports you spiritually is a spiritual practice, like meditation, that helps us practice this kind of un-attached giving. The idea being if you keep yourself in the flow there is always space for the new to come into your life.

Last week my granddaughter, Alex, and I were at the Children's Museum. There were lots of opportunities for me to remind Alex that we share with others. Sharing offers us opportunities to create connections, like Alex made playing with other children at the museum. We bring children into opportunity to share to teach how to make connections with others, to play nicely in groups.

So who do we give these riches to? Easy peasy. We give to what fills us, what supports us, what we love and what our heart is called to. I give to my spiritual community, Genesis, because it feeds me spiritually. I give to Safe Place women's shelter because I feel drawn to do so.

When we share our riches, time and talents with others we create friendships and alliances. Each interaction is like a beautiful thread which weaves friendships and bonds together. Thinking of it like this we are covered with fine threads that go out to every person in our lives.

Make a picture in your mind showing where your giving threads go. Amazing how many connections you have! You are an international connector, the beginning of your planetary work.

Much love,

Cathy

Eight

War

Dear Cathy,

Will people (in general) ever get to the point that they will see war as a sign of weakness?

Always,

Anna

Anna:

Do you mean will the idea that war is a sign of weakness ever be the prevailing idea on the planet? Maybe, but I think not. But do not despair over this.

Remember how we talked about the chakra system? The lower chakras are about survival, reproduction and the law. The idea of survival is a basic need for the continuation of the species. The concept that we will, as individuals, a community or larger tribe defend ourselves is a built in response of being human. These lower chakras are our basic instincts of survival. The upper chakras are about being an individual. Individual thought can only occur after those basic needs are met.

War outplays our need to meet these lower chakra needs. We have wars because somebody has something we want and we need it. Just like the children playing at the Children's Museum, we work out on a global scale that we need to share.

Having a monitor helps, offering solutions to the sharing dilemma like distractions, time outs and reasoning. Ultimately that external monitor/teacher has to become internalized. An internalized impulse control makes reasoned decisions over the "I need it and I want it now" part of us. We all have an entire chakra system that includes the lower chakras. We don't grow out of the lower community chakras into the upper personalized chakras; we are constantly working out the balance of the entire system.

The same is true for our family system, community system and global system. Our goal is not to see one aspect of our creation as a sign of weakness, but as an expression of the whole. I would hope we could reach a point where a majority of the individual, community and global systems reflect a mature balance of the "I want and need" to decisions based on the good of the whole.

In the chakra system the lower system in our physical bodies is the survival part, the upper physical is the personal and above that are the next level of chakras, the meta-physical or symbolic community. As we reach into this area of expression we incorporate our survival level, our personal and move into the transpersonal. Seeing ourselves as the larger Self we have been talking about. From this level we see that we are everything. From here we don't need something someone else has because we already have it, expressing through them.

Each of us is always working on the journey into these metaphysical realms. We individually and collectively will work out how to structure the world and how we live. A messy and wonderful affair.

So today find those places of war within yourself and find healing there. Everything is connected. Your inner work affects the entire picture.

Much love,
Cathy

Nine

Every family needs a contract

Greetings Anna!

We are so happy you are going to live with us this year! Below is a list of things we have been thinking about and discussing with your parents. This is not exactly a list of rules, but a fluid and open mutual agreement. Our main objective is to live with mutual respect and consideration for each other's space.

- Our house is open to you except our bedroom. Your bedroom and small bathroom is your private space and we will respect your privacy.

- If you have friends over you can use the recreation room or the living room. You will have more privacy in the rec room.

- I need a lot of time alone in my room or the living room. I am not always available for conversations. This does not mean I am sick; in fact I am taking a vacation from discussing my health. I would appreciate you deeply knowing I am well.

- Let us know if you need a heater, more blankets or a fan for your room.

- Eat whatever you want and clean up. Most evenings we fix dinner at home and you are always welcome to join us for meals. Please let us know if you are going to be home for meals or if you have a friend joining you.

- We would be happy to teach you how to cook and how to plan shopping so you have what you need and want in the kitchen.

- You can label your own food in the kitchen so we do not eat it – we will do the same if there is something we do not want you to eat.

- Have your own phone and computer.

- We will show you how to use our washer and dryer; we will provide the special soap needed for our washer.

- You can have a friend over while we are home. Between Sunday and Thursday they can stay until 11 p.m. and guests can stay later on Friday and Saturday nights. Please clear it with us for overnight guests--especially on week nights.

- We need things to wind down and be quiet in the house after 11 p.m. on weekdays. This includes outdoors.

- You can have a friend over when we are gone--you are in charge.

- You can use the rec room & blow up bed for overnight guests.

- The small bathroom is for you--please keep it cleaned up.

Keep all your things in your bedroom and bathroom.

- Let us know when to expect you home so we do not worry. We will do the same.

- We will keep our trip schedule updated so you know when we will be gone.

- We have an alarm system and arm it in the evenings and while we are gone. We will teach you how to use the alarm system.

- You need to make decisions based on what you know is appropriate for you. We are available for consult.

Call us for a ride if you or your driver is impaired. Even one drink is over the limit for driving under 21--what might be considered "social drinking" equals impaired driving. We are available for consult.

- No boys spending the night or at the house when we are not there. Please introduce us to your friends.

- Chuck and I will assist you to learn to drive. In the interim you will need to arrange rides, take the bus or bike. Usually Chuck works at the campus downtown and can give you a lift into town on weekdays if you would like.

Your parents are paying us for your room and board. In addition we expect you to do some housework in exchange for living with us. We have agreed that keeping up with the dishes and keeping the kitchen tidy will be your job. If we are entertaining, which we do often, we do not expect you to have to do all the clean up after the meal, others will pitch in to get the job done.

- We have visitors often, especially our kids and grandchildren. When they are here there will be times we want to hang out with them. Please ask if you can join us when we have company––the answer will usually be yes.

- No smoking of anything in or right around the house. You can use candles or incense in your room when you are home.

- No alcohol or drugs. This means not using alcohol or drugs at our home, having them in your room or on your person. This includes visiting friends.

- We will be available for family meetings to work out real life situations as they arise. You can ask for a meeting with us or we will ask for meetings with you.

- Do not build small fires in the living room and roast the squirrels. ;)

Love,

Cathy

Ten

Can you teach me to see fairies?

Dear Cathy,

Can you teach me how to see fairies?

Always,
Anna

Dear Anna:

I prefer the term "elementals," which refers to all types of earth-connected energies in the realm of the elements. Earth, Air, Fire and Water are all connected to the physical from the etheric realm. It is from the ethers that our connections to elementals emerge.

Flowers, trees, streams, crystals, stones, waterfalls, mountains, candle light, forest fires and all the others we share this planet with have a spirit connection. Fairies, sprites, undines, spirits called by many names exist in every part of the world, through every age, and in every language. They are our connection to elemental spirit. Here are some hints to seeing fairies:

- Wear clothing for outdoor weather.
- Start with a place that you feel is "magical", particularly in the deep woods or a field adjoining woods.
- Relax & get comfortable.
- Bring a gift (crystals, stone, fruit or flowers).

- Release preconceived ideas about what you are looking for (this isn't Disney's version of a fairy)!
- Relax your eyes and ears.
- Invite the elemental realm to show itself.
- Stay in the feeling realm instead of the thinking realm.
- Look for movement.
- Filter information about what you are seeing, feeling or hearing through your heart.
- Don't analyze, just watch.

There are already fairies around you and what you are doing. Here are some ideas if you want to draw these elementals into your yard:

- An "elemental area" brings together elements that fairies love--Earth, Fire, Water & Air.

- If possible choose a peaceful area away from dogs and cats.

- Create an area with low ground cover and dense shrubs.

- Place several low water containers such as clay tubs or bird baths.

- Include a bench or sitting log for you.

- Create a sacred circle marked with directional stones.

- Create a small altar (okay, the next chapter is about making an altar)!

Eleven

Our whole environment is an altar

Altars

Our whole environment is an altar. We all make choices about everything in our environment--what kind of drapes we have, what our couch looks like, what kind of pictures we hang on the wall. Our environment is a reflection of who we are. Creating a specific altar space is about bringing us into conscious awareness, so starting with a small place to create an altar is a really great way to begin to learn about this.

An altar sets an intention; it is like starting a machine that activates what your intention is. You can have a machine that is running full bore but you have to put it in gear before it can function.

Altars are very interactive. I do not have it set all the time in a particular way, I don't need to sit in front of it as my place to pray or meditate. Altars are for you to use in the way you want to. My process is playing with the creation of sacred space.

An altar is anything placed with intention. Just a few stones can be an altar. I can take stones from along my way on a walk, and hold them and center myself for a moment. As I place them down I will speak my intention. It doesn't have to even be out loud or the perfect words. I might say, "This is for balance in the physical, emotional, mental and spiritual body," and place them on top of each other. And that is an altar. So it can be really easy. The activation came in placing the stones together.

On my altar I have fire (a candle); I have water in a small bowl, earth with all the stones I have placed around, and air represented by a bell. I am intentionally thinking about the elements, bringing in the mix of what represents the planet. I put a representation of a deity of some kind, a god or goddess, on the altar.

Deities are aspects of the divine. When you use a deity, think of what you know of the qualities of that deity. Green Tara represents healing and Kuan Yin can represent compassion. You do not have to use a statue of a deity. Use something from nature that represents something to you, like a rose to represent love or healing.

I also have some of my own personal healing tools. I rarely use tools in my healing work but healing tools on my altar are a reminder of the reality of healing.

Years ago I was given a vision of a Druid woman working with a crystal. As the story was being told to me I could feel exactly what that crystal would have felt like in my hand and within a couple of weeks this crystal had been given to me.

I keep this crystal on my altar as a reminder of the power of intention.

I place my healing tools on my altar because it is a healing altar; I am going to place my tools there as a representation of healing, to empower them and to represent my healing journey.

Placing jewelry or personal items on the altar activates them. You can continue to add things or take things off the altar as you wish. With altars we are looking at the symbols and the rituals around the intention. A symbolic representation here of what is important to you.

Altar Care and Feeding

Tobacco is a spirit gift I always place on the altar. In some cultures they add wine or beer to the altar.

I always add chocolate to my altar. Care and feeding and also play. Adding chocolate is about how much fun the Divine could possibly have. So if I were a Divine being, which I am, then I would want someone to put chocolate on my altar. Hugs and Kisses are actually the kind of candy I chose to be on the altar, sweet and shiny!

Anything shiny activates. I have some small gold metal stars, just thrown around. I have a small mirror and small plastic mirror type jewels that can be bought at any craft store. These are great activators; anything shiny is "spirit attraction," mirrors, Christmas lights or candles.

Then I take a piece of paper and write a little affirmation. I write out what I want. I am going to put this in presence tense. An example of an affirmation I would use is "Divine Intelligence flows through me now."

Any time you have anything that smokes like incense, or sage, it is a bridge to Spirit. If you use incense or sage, it doesn't mean you are more holy if you use a lot. It is the intention of what you are doing, so a little tiny bit works as well as enough to set off fire alarms. If you use a shell to burn sage in make sure you don't put it down someplace where it could burn what it's sitting on. I use is a small brass container with sand in it.

If you are in an area where you can't use something that smokes or people have sensitivities, please don't think you are not being holy if you can't use it. There are lots of ways to clear energetics in the space.

I activate my altar with rice or white corn meal. I throw it as hard as I can towards the altar, so it bounces around. So now I have turned the key on, activating the altar. Just using your intention can activate the altar, but using some sort of ritual works really well.

So what if I blow the candle out before I go to bed? When I re-light the candle the next day will I have reactivated the altar all over again? It is the question I had as a child going into church. There was a light that was always lit signifying that God was present. I used to think God was present because the candle was lit. If the candle blew out would God leave? Of course it is your intention that keeps the altar active, not that a candle is lit. The altar is always activated. Lighting the candle reactivates you.

Love,

Cathy

Twelve

Melba Wisdom

Dear Anna,

Have I ever told you about Chuck's Aunt Melba? I call what I learned from her "Melba Wisdom".

Melba came into my life shortly after Chuck's mom Edna was diagnosed with ovarian cancer. Although I had met her years before on a whirlwind tour of western Colorado, I cannot clearly remember that meeting.

Melba's relationship to Chuck's family was by marriage to an uncle living at great distance. The possibility of our paths ever crossing at all was remote; that she entered my life was truly a blessing.

Melba moved into my in-law's house to care for Edna. She fixed the meals, kept the house, bathed her, and generally helped out. This was not the first time Melba had played this role. She had helped many loved ones through terminal

illness. Her purpose went way beyond caring for Edna.
She really cared for us all as we tried to prepare for Edna's
transition. She was always available with a cup of tea, a hug
and time to listen.

I have to admit I almost missed the opportunity to learn
and accept love from her. Melba was soft and round. She
wore polyester pants, and seldom wore her false teeth. She
was raised in a small town and has been a care giver of one
type or another all her life. The kind of person, much to
my chagrin, I might not have seen. She was simply, and
profoundly, fully herself in every situation. This is what I call
"Melba Wisdom."

There was a shine about her and sparkle of Spirit that
outward appearance could not conceal. My first lesson
was to really see her, and to keep seeing the real Edna as
her physical appearance deteriorated so quickly. Melba
encouraged us to say what we needed to say, to express our
love to Edna and to risk not pulling back. Melba was quick
to hug and quicker to laugh deeply. Many times Melba cried
with us. She encouraged us to keep Edna's bedroom full of
grandchildren playing. She took time to let us speak our
sorrow. Melba said "Just love each other."

Now I am always on the lookout for Melbas in every person I meet. I approach each encounter knowing that everyone holds their own brand of Melba Wisdom and it is my job to find that wisdom in each person. Then it hit me that I hold Melba Wisdom too! Today I am always at the ready with a cup of tea, a hug, and most importantly, I am available to listen.

May I stay vigilant and not overlook any form through which Spirit moves and not judge by outside appearance. May I recognize my teacher in every person I meet. Let me continue to risk love without fear of being left alone. Let me give voice to what is in my heart and listen from a place of healing. May I honor Spirit in simplicity.

Just be about love,

Cathy

Thirteen

I am not sure I believe in God.

Dear Cathy,

I am so glad you are taking time to answer all my questions. I have a confession to make. I am not sure I even believe there is a God. Is something wrong with me? What do you actually believe?

Anna

Oh Sweetie, there is nothing wrong with you!

It is perfectly normal for a teenager to question if there is a God. In fact, good for you! As a child we are raised in our family religion, if they have one, and exposed to ideas our parents want for us. As we grow and start to form our own ideas it is important to let go of our predetermined beliefs and explore what is real for us.

I actually don't believe in God either, if you are talking about some guy sitting on a cloud. I don't even believe there is some outside force that punishes or rewards our behavior.

My Mother freaked when I left the Catholic Church as a teenager. The church I was raised in just didn't fit for me anymore; especially the "women can't be priests" thing. Oh, and the church being against a woman's right to choose.

Explore lots of different religions, life philosophies and begin to formulate what you believe in. I explored several different religions after leaving the church. I had a brief "born again" phase, then went into a prolonged "Church of the Divine Sunday Brunch" period where the extent of my spiritual life was a good long breakfast and the newspaper on Sundays.

What I believe is that we are all part of the creation. The force that grows and continues is infinite and divine. The word God is a way of saying that "All is One", it is everything, the big YES, the source of creative flow. You can call is whatever you want, you can just call it love. There is no way to be separated from this flow of YES, nothing you can do to separate yourself from that good.

Oh, and this flow of creation is there for you if you believe it or not!

Be good to yourself, be good to others and to the planet. Follow your heart, it will always lead you in the right direction.

In grace,

Cathy

Fourteen

Why do people have disabilities?

Dear Cathy,

Can I ask you about why people have disabilities? If we choose what we are going to learn in our life, why would someone choose to be disabled? That does not make sense to me.

Anna

Greetings Anna:

We all come into our human experience with a specific path of learning, a spiritual quest so to speak. In some people this "charism" or imbuement by God comes in the form of what they actually end up doing for their living or through some event that touches this person during their time here. For some of us it is not as clear as what we do for a living or how we can communicate or even what we can think.

Helen Keller was a great communicator. In terms of reincarnation she probably had many life times where she was a great speaker and communicator. In this last incarnation with communication being her deep charism, on a soul level, she made a decision to push her gifts as a great communicator to the limit. I am not saying she in fact chose her inability to hear, speak or talk (although later in her life she did verbalize in private) but she did utilize her disability as a way to forward her charism. We are all given a choice of how we will utilize the specific gifts we are given.

This question of how disabilities figure into our spiritual growth is very important to me because of the car crash our family was in. This crash (I do not believe in accidents) deeply and profoundly impacted me on all levels and 20 surgeries later I continue to deal with the physical, mental and emotional effects.

Disabilities seem to bring us into precise living. Many levels of what other people deal with become unimportant; others become very important. It appears the more we block out input and stresses or normal day to day life, the opportunity to fine tune into an area that others would not go increases.

In my own life I practice every day being in gratitude for where I am and practice letting go of the things I can no longer do. I focus on the fact that I know I myself have entered this advanced schooling of my "disability" for the express purpose of becoming totally present, and in that presence becoming the flow of the Divine I know myself to be. It stops being about what we do, but how we be.

Love,

Cathy

Touch Drawing

Fifteen

Can you take me to see a ghost?

Dear Cathy,

Can you take me to see a ghost?

Anna

Anna:

Do you want to experience a ghost for yourself? The Olympia Hotel, home of the Urban Onion, is a great haunted space. Here is my true tale of The Haunted Bathroom.

I was eating lunch at the Urban Onion downtown. I had to go to the bathroom so I got the key and headed downstairs. I went into a stall and had started to go when I heard the bathroom door open and someone come in.

If you have been in this bathroom you know there are three stalls. I was in the one to the far left and the person who came in went into the stall at the far right. I remember listening to the shuffle of an older woman and the smell of her flowery perfume. I heard her open the door to the stall and sit down.

I didn't hear noises from the stall the old woman had entered so being a curious girl I leaned down and looked under the stall door. No shoes. That's more than a little weird, I thought to myself. Maybe she is sitting with her feet up on the seat.

I finished my business and came out to wash my hands. Now I was very curious so I touched the door and it swung open. There was no one there.

The bathroom is so small she could not have slipped out undetected. Yikes! I finished up quickly and opened the door to leave the bathroom. I stopped and turned around looking back at the stalls. The toilet in the last stall flushed. I was out of there!

Seeing energy is actually quite simple. Here is the technique I use to see auras and spirits.

- Get into a comfortable and relaxed position.

- Feel a connection to the center of the earth.

- Imagine you can open the top of your head and feel a connection to Spirit.

- Let go of any expectations you have about what or how spirits appear.

- Breathe deeply and feel yourself relaxing and expanding with each breath.

- Open your eyes and relax your focus. Use soft vision rather than trying to look at details.

- Repeat.

If you ask someone who can see spirits what they see they will give you all sorts of answers. Some people see spirits like real people while others see movement or feel an emotion. Sometimes there is a picture inside your head, not an actual vision. There always is a feeling, an emotional echo, that lingers. Saying "I see" often means "I feel and perceive." Trust what you see and perceive. Like any skill, being able to see spirits gets stronger as you practice. Remember ALL is One, so is nothing separate from you; it is all an aspect of the Divine.

In grace,
Cathy

Sixteen

Looking for Casper

Okay, since we are on the subject of ghosts, here is an article I wrote about poltergeists for the <u>Sitting Duck</u> newspaper in Olympia! The article is a response to the following question from a reader:

Dear Cathy:

I'm planning on having a haunted house this Halloween, and I would like to use real poltergeists. Is there any way I can temporarily bring poltergeists into my house for the holidays?

Signed,

Looking for Casper

Dear Looking:

I am glad you have asked me this question. This important holiday information was not even mentioned in Martha Stewart's special Halloween addition of her magazine!

Most people get confused about the different hauntings available. If you are looking for something along the lines of a shrieking form holding its head and walking down the hall you are actually looking for a repetitive image haunting. This is the kind of ghostly occurrence which repeats the same sequence over and over again. These instant replay ghosts are like looking at a tape recording of high intensity emotion. This is why these images are often associated with grief and trauma. In Bellingham there is a hotel where you can hear a man pacing and a woman screaming in pain where a woman died in childbirth. In my house a woman repeatedly comes down a stairwell and puts away laundry in a cupboard. Neither the stairs nor the cupboard currently exists in the house. I don't know what her great trauma was but she is an intent housekeeper. I have however been unable to get her to also fold my clothes while in this state of angst.

If you are looking for the interactive variety of haunting this becomes a bit more complicated. An aspect or fragment of the person does not go into the light and they avoid the "other-side welcoming committee" which comes to pick them up. This can happen because they have unfinished business, died in a confused state or because they have a feeling they are going to hell for stealing that eraser in 4th grade. Often they will stay connected to their house and think they are still the owners. Some are gracious hosts and some want you out.

The E.R. Rodgers restaurant in Steilacoom is a great example of both types of ghosts. My father grew up next door to the house that has served as a private residence, boarding house and now a restaurant. He had many stories about the "ghost with red eyes" looking out the front windows of the house overlooking the water. Recently I was walking into the downstairs women's bathroom and actually excused myself and moved to the side as an upset woman in a long taffeta dress cut directly in front of me hurrying to some unknown destination, disappearing into the bathroom wall. The interactive ghost, a scruffy old man, resides upstairs and stands on the stairs and harasses the restaurant guests and staff, turning lights on and off and moving things around in the kitchen. You can often smell his pipe smoke upstairs in the late evening. I understand nobody wants the job of being the last one out.

If you would like a list of some of the other haunted places you can go online to find more local haunts.

If you are looking for a true poltergeist experience (poltergeist means "to knock" and "spirit" in German), I have two words--adolescent girls. Loud knocking, objects moving about on their own, voices, particular odors and apparitions are the hallmark of poltergeist experiences. These experiences tend to focus around a preteen female whose hormones and the stress of that age combine and finally release subconsciously in flinging dishes and loud rappings. Activity has also been associated with much stressed teens and young adults of either sex but there is nothing like a group of 14-year-old girls to stir up a bit of Halloween haunting. The energies surrounding adolescence are very powerful forces.

In other times and cultures, young adults were initiated into adulthood and taught skills to begin to run energy through their bodies and direct these emerging energies into effective creative forces. Today's adolescents move into this energetically powerful time unassisted by the older wise ones in the village and end up flinging things through the air willy-nilly. This might be a little disconcerting for the family down the block, but can assist you wonderfully in creating the atmosphere you desire for that special Halloween effect. Be sure to get a note from the girl's parents before proceeding.

Place four agitated teens in the corners of the room and for best results keep large amounts of Halloween snack-sized Snickers bars close at hand. Encourage them to look in the mirror by candlelight, repeating the name "Bloody Mary" until totally worked up. Place an assortment of small, easy-to-fling objects in the center of the room, and enjoy!

Cathy

Seventeen

Could you see things as a child?

Dear Cathy,

Could you see things when you were a child? Did you know what you wanted to be when you grew up?

Anna

Anna:

Being a good Catholic girl, I have early childhood memories of attending mass. I would watch the priests as they stood before the congregation in their beautiful robes. The smell of incense filled my nostrils. The part I looked forward to the most was the moment the priest turned his back to us to cast his magical spell over the bread and wine. I watched as the spiraling energy expanded around him. The front of the church would be filled with movement and light. Then he would turn and hold up this wondrous transformed substance. I recognized myself in the energy that was present around the priest and I knew who I was. I knew I was that energy. Because the only place I saw this transformation occur was in the church I was very clear this was my path. I knew I was to be a priest.

At the age of four, I would set up the garage at home into my sanctuary. A 2x4 became the communion rail. I brought my menagerie of stuffed animals and dolls into this holy place. I carefully squished Wonder Bread between my little hands and used a small round cookie cutter to make the hosts.

I began the magic. Lights swirled around me. I felt bigger than life and for a moment I was raised above the roofline. "This is my body," I cried out, "This is my blood." The transformation was real.

My mother walked in while the teddy bears were receiving their communion. "Isn't that cute! Cathy is playing mass!" Then she said the words that would change the next 35 years of my life: "Maybe you want to be a nun when you grow up? Girls cannot be priests." What!!!

I saw that the nuns, at least the ones I knew then, did not hold the same ability to transform in the way I saw at mass. I was sure some mistake had been made and an exception would be made for me.

So yes, I have always been able to see things. I thought it meant I was supposed to be a priest since that is where I saw all the energy. It was not until I was older that I began to see it around other powerful people, even women! I began to see that in a way I AM a priest, just not the kind I thought I would be!

Cathy

Eighteen

Source creates and discovers itself

Dear Cathy,

Do we choose the exact date we are born?
Do we choose the exact date and way we die?

So if this "source" is always trying to break
off into other forms of life to create and discover
itself, then does it have to fold into separation?
Does this "source" have to make examples of
what it does not want to be like? Or is this only
more of a human goal?

Anna

Dear Anna,

My goodness, I did say you could ask me anything! Okay.

Have you seen pictures from an electron microscope? Pictures from the Hubble space telescope? Notice how there is a similar look to them? Notice how the macro and micro world have a similar look.

Fractals are another way to look into the complex and connected nature of our world.

"Because they appear similar at all levels of magnification, fractals are often considered to be infinitely complex (in informal terms). Natural objects that approximate fractals to a degree include clouds, mountain ranges, lightning bolts, coastlines, and snowflakes." (*Wikipedia*)

If you think about creative force, the big "Yes" wave that travels into and through all things big and little, there are two factors--particles and waves. Two forms of the same thing depending on how it is observed.

These heady pieces of information, fractals, particles and waves are the nearest things we have in the physical world to explain the connectedness in all things. In terms of quantum physics, this is the meeting between scientific understanding and spiritual knowing.

Again we go back to the "All is Now" in answering your questions about life and death. How old are you really, Anna?!

In the wave of creative force we already exist and will always remain within that creative momentum.

This dimension has a creation wave; our cadre, or group, has a creation wave and each being has a creation wave. The duality needed to see us as separate from the One force creates a counter balance to the wave's motion.

Moving in and out of body is very much like surfing. Waves come in groups; several small waves then the big wave. You can come to shore on any wave you choose but that big wave gives you the momentum to go farther and faster if you can figure out when to go. Plus there are other surfers waiting with a similar mission.

Everything is part of this pattern of creative flow. People figured out long ago they could read the pattern of this flow in the stars. I believe with skill anyone can read the pattern in anything. For example I once did a "reading" based on the french fries left on a person's plate. It is all there; you just need to know how to look!

Because we are One and All is Now the comings and goings into and out of bodies is simply part of the continuing whole. I have so far witnessed many births, over 200, and about 10 deaths. Every one was amazing.

Without exception souls catch the wave that brings them into their highest expression and leave with the same enthusiasm.

Cathy

Nineteen

What exactly is an aura?

Dear Cathy,

What exactly is an aura? Why are some different than others?

Do we make or choose our auras? What do they say about us? Are auras and chakras the same thing?

Anna

Oh Anna! You are so curious!

An aura is fields of subtle, luminous radiation surrounding a person or object like the halo around a saint in old religious art. Some people think the aura or halo around a saint means they are particularly special or holy. Really everybody has one; it is just a layer of energy that extends out beyond the physical body.

Through many ages people have tried to interpret what the aura means. According to different spiritual groups such as Theosophy and Anthroposophy, each color of the aura has a precise meaning indicating a precise emotional state. A complete description of the aura and its colors was provided by Charles Leadbeater, a theosophist of the 19th century. He was not the first to note the colors and their meaning but he is a great place to start if you want to learn more.

Auras are one of those things that are hotly debated, and everyone has an opinion and a theory about what it all means. What I know is most people can see auras. Usually they begin by seeing shades of gray and small movements.

Going back to All is One (are you sick of that answer yet?!) remember I come from the idea that there is no separation. Our physical bodies are just one aspect of our nature and of our creation. Each thought and idea we create vibrates at a certain level.

Our physical body is a complex organ on every level. Every organ, our skin, our brain, everything has its own set of complex and multilevel understanding. Our physical bodies are arranged to assist us in our human experience.

We begin with our personal survival, our need to reproduce the species and to form bonds in community. Those bonds start with our family and start to include a bigger group as we grow and evolve. Being part of the group is integral to our survival and wellbeing. On this level of creation we are a group assisting each other out of the need for the group to survive. If we need meat for the village a group can go out and hunt and bring back food for the group. The group survival is what it is about.

In the body these functions of survival and reproduction are in the lower half of the body. Nerve bundles from the base of the spine wrap around the body, transmitting signals from the brain (and other areas in the chest and belly). Those nerve bundles pulse with energy, a kind of electrical energy that surround and amplify the body to do what is needed. This is why sex is such a strong and pervasive urge, our prime directive, so to speak.

Chakra means "energy wheel." These energy wheels are actually in the same place that there are physical nerve bundles branching into bigger nerve bundles that go up our spine and into our head. A kind of radar system that covers many levels of input.

Lower chakras are ruled by the idea of survival, reproduction and community. They correspond to the ideas held about "Aries," which are about creating laws for community wellbeing and holding those laws firmly.

So if the hunters in our village decide to go for a dip in the lake instead of bringing home meat, some hungry and angry people would meet them. The answer "because we just felt like it" does not fly within this structure. Can you think of some groups/organizations that rely on thinking like this? Where the importance of thinking as a group outweighs the self? We never grow out of this kind of thinking but have found ways to create laws and groups that might take into consideration both the group and the self.

The upper part of the body does think of the self and could make the decision not to bring back the meat. This individualized thought comes from a higher consciousness based on our own needs and not the group. The 3rd chakra, in the belly, is our "feeling" sense. Again, nerves wrap around from the spine and create this place to feel our emotions and make decisions based on how we feel. From here it makes perfect sense to spend all our money on that great pair of shoes instead of our rent, because we feel like it.

Working from this level we can begin to make balanced decisions based on all our needs.

Then there is the heart chakra which is about love, but not so much "in love" personal love, but a bigger expansion into understanding the One.

The 5th chakra is the throat chakra. This is about speaking your truth and in a deeper way balancing the personal self with the Divine.

The 6th chakra is the middle of the head. It is the spiritual driver's seat of the body. The 7th chakra on the top of the head is the receiver. All the upper chakras, 4 to 7, are self-individualized and associated with Pisces.

All the chakras above are in the symbolic realm of Aquarius. The study of the chakra system can take lifetimes. I am glad you asked me about chakras and auras together because they are connected.

Each of the resonate bodies represented by the chakra system vibrate around the body. Starting with the 1st chakra and going out and beyond the 8th we are a vibrating field of energy. These fields shift with our thoughts and ideas and what is going on emotionally and physically and can be influenced by the people who surround us.

Because I do not see things as "good or bad," simply aspects of the Divine manifesting, all these influences become an amazing display around the physical body.

You have to develop your own way of interpreting what you are seeing. The more you study and experience looking at auras, the more you will grow in your understanding.

For example, I knew a certain pattern of numbers and symbols equaled the color blue. And I interpreted that as blue for many years. One day it just became the color blue (whatever that means)! So I think we are always interpreting information based on our connection.

Auras shift and change all the time. It is easiest to see auras in partial darkness and in front of a plain background. Stripes or patterns behind the person you are looking at will make it harder to see an aura. All kinds of things, even taking deep breaths or taking a drink of water changes how big and bright an aura can get. I can make my aura really big and I can shift into energetic animal shapes. Practice my dear, practice!

In grace,

Cathy

Twenty

Aquarian Cookie

Dear Cathy,

What is the Aquarian Age? Are
we in it now? Is something going to
happen?

Anna

Anna:

Here is a reading for you: Hmm, let's see . . . "This last year has been filled with huge and unexpected events. Old health issues have risen to the surface. You have stopped dreaming. On a deep level you are reassessing who you are and what you're about. You have entered uncharted territory and it is a bit scary. It feels like you are waiting for something to happen." How do I know this? Welcome my friend to the Age of Aquarius. You are made for this time.

There is a lot of discussion about the new age and entering the Age of Aquarius and the whole end-of-the-earth thing. I can with all assurance say we are no longer waiting for the big event to happen, it has happened. The Aquarian cookies have been baking and they have just been pulled from the oven.

To catch you up on the "Ages" thing, when the Babylonians calculated the zodiac the vernal equinox was in Aries. The Age of Aries was all about forming the law and strengthening tribal connections. At the beginning of the Common Era, "A.D.", we shifted into the Age of Pisces. The Age of Pisces, represented by the fish, was about sacrifice and self-individualization. Each cycle represents a teaching that is imbued into the fabric of humankind. Kind of a "lesson plan" of where we are headed.

The Age of Aquarius has been "downloading"

information for some time. The total download has occurred this year. As we go through this change we are not just affected on a planetary level, but within our communities, our families and personally. We hold the cycle that affects the entire planet in our bodies. Our personal evolution can be tracked through the chakra system.

One of my favorite teachers is Carolyn Myss. I studied with Carolyn and learned all about the different "Ages," like Aquarius, as they are represented in the body.

The chakra system acts as an energetic marker beginning at the base of the spine, up through our body and beyond. Each one of us goes through these developmental markers as we mature in our lives. The lower chakra system, below the waist, is about the tribal and group consciousness. As children we are totally involved with this level. It is a normal occurrence for teens and young adults to begin to self-individualize and move above the waist, into the exploration of self in the upper chakra system.

With the Age of Pisces coming to a close we have now traveled through the entire body system. With the beginning of the Age of Aquarius we are ready to explore the world of the invisible. The Age of Aquarius is about archetypal thinking and global consciousness. Aquarius is an air sign, filled with exploration of science and new inventions. We have entered the realm of connectedness.

So why are we struggling? Didn't we think we would go lightly into this new age? Brotherhood and understanding? Sympathy and trust abounding? And yet our planet, countries, communities, families and we are searching for balance. The only way to do this is to realign with the new level. At the beginning of every era there is a "reset" that occurs, seating the new teaching level into each chakra from the 1st upwards. Just when we think we have reached great enlightenment at the close of an age, we begin again with survival. There is a sense of something dying and things falling away. We are releasing old thoughts and ideas and how they have been created over the last 2000 years in religions, countries, communities and families and within ourselves. You can figure out by looking around what the result of this level of "reset" can lead to. People are in love with power and control and do not give up the reins so easily.

As our bodies now move to this new vibration, anything that is held in an old belief pattern, which still vibrates at the old level, is now out of alignment with the new Aquarian pattern. Anything coming up for you this year around physical health, relationships or however else you are manifesting is directly related to holding a group of old thoughts and beliefs around that system.

So now what? We have been downloading bits of this new age since about the 60's. There are groups of people who have formed new thinking patterns and are now assisting others through this shift. These forerunners have paved the way for us, creating paths that can assist us in unfolding gently into this new age.

It appears many of these early workers, healers and spiritual teachers are being hit especially hard right now. Within this group we are not receiving "Aquarian 101" lessons, but rather we are being asked to defend our thesis.

It is all about being in the moment. It is only in the present that we can make the shifts necessary. The good news is that whatever beliefs are not in alignment will become visible. Your area of teaching will be springing forth for you to uncover and bring into alignment. And the readjustment of whatever that is can happen in one moment. We have entered the time of the expanded self, the time of instant manifestation, the age of miracles. Whatever has arisen for you, the solution truly lies within, between the breaths, ready for you to claim. And the best news is you do not have to do it yourself because this is the age of global community.

Oh, and remember that each age lasts about 2000 years so we have plenty of time to figure this all out. In the movie *The Matrix*, the Oracle talks to Neo about his future, which seems bigger than he can handle. She says "eat this cookie, by the time you are finished, you will be right as rain."

Be peace. All is One. All is Now.
Cathy

P.S.

If you are interested in learning more about the effects of astrology on a personal and planetary level I would recommend *The Only Astrology Book You'll Ever Need,* by Joanna Martine Woolfolk. For more information about the connection of the ages to the chakra system I recommend *Anatomy of Spirit,* by Carolyn Myss.

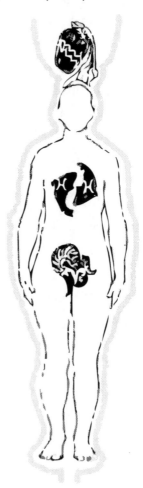

Twenty-one

Be still enough to hear a duck at your door

Anna, on a lighter note, let's talk about careful listening.

Some years ago, in a time of magic much like now, I lived in a house near a lake. I was a young mother then with a toddler and a preschooler. As I worked around the house on a particularly beautiful spring day, I heard a strange sound coming from outside. I went to the front door and there on the stoop stood a duck.

Although to my knowledge I had never actually conversed with a duck, there I was. Her quacking and clucking gave way to understanding of why she was there. She expressed her displeasure for having to seek out human help, but a stronger interspecies tie of motherhood had drawn us together. At her urging I followed her around to the back of the house. "See, there they are," mother duck exclaimed. "I don't know how this happened," she said. "They were with me one moment, and the next, well, there they are!" Sure enough, there they were––ten little ducklings, squawking and hopping madly, stuck down in the crawl space beside the house.

By this time quite a crowd was gathering. Children

from all over the neighborhood rushed to the scene, all wanting to see the baby ducklings up close. This further flustered momma duck, and I shooed the children back to the fence to watch from a respectful distance. The children thought nothing of me conversing out loud with a duck, perfectly natural.

There was a busy street between our house and the lake. I was afraid if I just took the ducklings out they would never make it across the road. "I'm going for a box," I told the momma duck.

Returning with a box from the garage, I carefully picked up each baby until I placed them all into the box. The babies yelled "Momma!" and momma yelled back, "It's all right, she's trying to help!"

"OK, they are in the box, now show me were to go," I said. Momma duck was off, first flying, and then walking directly in front of me, quacking out "this way, and "just a little farther," and exclaiming that we would be there now if only I could fly.

Down the street in procession we went, momma duck, me with the box full of squeaking babies, and the whole group of children, both walking and on tricycles, singing "We're taking the babies home!"

As we all carefully crossed the street and headed up the grassy hill leading to the lake, momma duck told me this was far enough. I put the box down and tipped it over so the baby ducks could hop out. They all ran straight to their mother, where she kissed and scolded them saying, "Now stay close, and don't wander about!" And off they went, momma duck leading the way and all the ducklings in a line behind her.

The children and I watched as they disappeared down the hill. We turned and headed back for home when suddenly above our heads circled mamma duck! "Thank you! Thank you!" and off she flew to rejoin her babies.

Spring surrounds us now. The promise of renewal unfolds around us. This is a time to breathe deeply, become aware of the small details in nature and rejoice in relationships with others, even those who appear quite different from us. Spring is the time to open our hearts wide, and honor Spirit flowing through everything, connecting us in a way so even humans and ducks can speak to each other. We are all one.

May you be still enough inside to hear a duck at your door. Blessings.

Cathy

Twenty-two

Night School

Dear Cathy,

Is 4 a.m. a special time of the day? Why? What is Night School?

Anna

Dear Anna:

Since 1988 I have been attending a series of special classes in my dreams. I have graduated from four separate "Night Universities" and today continue taking special classes, but primarily I teach and do healing work in my dreams.

The dreams began shortly after my spiritual awakening in 1988. I had a near-death experience after my family was involved in a car crash. Because of internal injuries I had emergency surgery that left an incision from pelvic bone to sternum. I woke in the hospital with several light beings around my bed. They had long delicate fingers that seemed to weave the air above my stomach. Explaining to me the surgeon had done all he could to repair the damage, they began the delicate work of repairing the field above my body. I thought they were playing the piano. "We will show you this technique later," they said. And they kept their promise. The first healing technique I was taught in night school was how to extend my fingers into long beams of light that could knit together what appeared to me as a multi-layered grid surrounding the body.

School has always occurred between 12:00 a.m. and 4:45 a.m. "Night School" dreaming begins after a short period of regular dreams that often intertwines the day's events or situations. School often begins with an experience of traveling. When my night studies began in 1988, every dream began in the same way. I would be propelled through a tunnel of light. As time went on I became very curious and wanted to learn more about the tunnel. I learned to slow down and actually look at the tunnel. It was math formulas and geometric shapes. I have always thought it humorous that this piece of information would be revealed to me since I have always had such trouble with numbers. The secret of the "tunnel formula" is definitely safe with me.

On the other end of the tunnel was always a park-like setting with a carved stone bench and a water fountain. A teacher would come towards me and we would walk or sit together and discuss what the class was to be about. My first classes were the longest, sometimes lasting several months on one concept. Other times a lesson would happen in one night. As I learned about one subject I would be offered opportunities in waking state following the teaching to test out the level of my new understanding.

I had been going to the temple courtyard in my dreams for over a year when I attended a slide presentation of sacred sites. One of the slides showed my bench. I got so excited I had the woman giving the presentation go back to the slide so I could really look at the picture. I explained the temple building to the side of the bench, the fountain and the hills surrounding them. "It is exactly as you are saying. So you have been to Malta?" she asked. "Yes," I answered, "last night in my dream I was there in class." In my dream my Malta classroom is a thriving present time reality. The fountain bubbles and it is lush and green.

My first two years in night school were just like waking state. There was always a physical setting, like the Malta temple, and human beings. As time went on school became much more complicated. I began to experience myself and the other participants in different forms, such as dolphin-like beings, feline-looking "lion persons." The form I take most frequently now is as a very tall light being. I realized if my teachers would have started with these images it would have been too much for my sleepy humanness to take in. I am always grateful to my teachers for the gentle way they allowed me to grow. I strive to offer my students, both in day school and night school, the same gift.

Now my experience in night school varies depending on what I am doing. Sometimes the dreams begin with a meeting with other beings. Sometimes I go directly to a place and begin to work with someone. When I first began to receive teachings I thought all the teachers I worked with were angels or guides. As my work has grown to include doing teaching and healing in dreams, I now appear as that same kind of teacher I believed to be Angels.

Often my night school travels take me to a real earth location. I belong to a group of beings that work regularly on a tall narrow pyramid in Guatemala. From the top of this location I work with energies which are connected around the planet between this pyramid and other sacred sites. This next spring I will be traveling in waking state to visit this site.

Sometimes the people I work with in dreamtime find me. A woman came into my office for an appointment. She began to cry as she came in. She said she had a very difficult period the month before and had prayed for an angel to help her. I had appeared in her dream comforting her and told her to "go see Cathy Pfeil." I even spelled my name out for her explaining it was a difficult spelling. She was very surprised to find her special angel was a regular person! I asked her what I was wearing in the dream and she described a new dress I had recently purchased. In her dream I appeared exactly as I am in waking life.

In dream state I created myself the same, no beautiful long legged body, no thick wavy hair, just me. I asked my night school teachers why I would do that if I could create myself any way I wanted in dreams. "You can create yourself any way you want in dream state, but you can in your waking life too", he said. "You are completely your manifestation."

Without fail as soon as night school ends I wake up. Waking up seems to be a method I use to help me remember my lessons. I then fall back to sleep and spend from 4:45 to the time I wake up in the morning taking specific questions into dream and receiving answers. I wake and sleep in cycles that allow me to maintain a lucid interactive state. I ask questions about the teachings I am receiving and about things happening in my personal life. I also spend time in active prayer and healing for people who have asked me to do long distance work with them.

I remember my dreams as if they are waking state. To me everything that happens in my dreams is as real as what happens in my waking life. One of the impacts this has had on my life is the realization that waking state is as richly symbolic as dream state. In my dream state I am involved in a moving tapestry of images and teachings in which I interact. I now live in my waking life in a tapestry of images I interact with at the same level of lucidity and conscious creation.

If I have trouble interpreting what just happened or it seems too complicated, I ask for the teaching again in a simpler form. I know the next dream will be the simpler version. If I still don't understand I keep asking for simpler dreams until it is clear. Then the dreams reverse and become more complicated until I am back at the original dream.

I keep a journal of my dreams and reread them frequently. As I continue to grow and change the level at which I understand, the dreams increase. I have found dream interpretation books of little help in understanding my own dreams. Exploring my own dreams and what the symbols mean for me has been the best dream interpretation tool.

Moving from one "Night University" into another often includes a completion dream. I enjoy playing in my life, and my dream life is no different. A good completion dream for me needs all the trimmings--a final "Ah-ha!" experience, receiving a grade, a gold crown and a party.

Here is one of my completion dreams:

I had gone to a workshop. I was late getting there because I was teaching a class. I arrived just as the group was getting ready to walk down to another location near the water to continue their work. The woman and man who were leading the group handed me a small pouch with what I thought were Tarot cards, but I did not look.

I put the pouch down by my luggage and began to talk to the man and woman about what the class had been doing. They told me each group was setting their own criteria for the class and everyone already had partners except two. There was a woman who was working on issues concerning women and babies and a man working on understanding Kundalini energy. I told them I would work with the man because I had already completed my studies on women and children.

I went to pick up my pouch and join the group when I saw it was missing. The instructors would not let me join the class without my bag and they all went on without me.

I began to search for my pouch. I was then in my own house and searched everywhere. There were great piles of art supplies and ritual objects under beds, in closets, everywhere. I looked in every place there was to look but could not find the pouch. I could hear the group drumming and singing and could see them when I looked out the window. I felt angry and frustrated.

Finally I decide I was going anyway. As I was leaving the house I heard a piano playing very softly "Heart and Soul." I went back into the house and there was a little spirit girl with dark hair and eyes at the piano. I went up to her and sat down on the bench. "It was so pretty." she said. "I wanted it for myself, so I took it." She pointed to the pouch on the top of the piano.

"How about if I make you another just like it?" I asked. "I will begin working on it tonight and complete it a bit at a time until it is done, and you give me the bag so I can join the class?"

Two older spirit children appeared––an older brother and sister. "That is a great idea," they said. I took the bag and for the first time opened it. Inside was a set of Tarot cards, but they were all blank.

I took the cards in the pouch and joined the class just as they were finishing. I was still thinking about the girl and the cards and wanted to share what had happened. I told the male instructor the story of the little spirit girl. He asked, "Do you know what goes on the cards now?" I said, "Yes, half would be in-breaths and half would be out-breaths. The in-breath cards would all have adventures and events that have happened to me which I have created on my path. The out-breath cards would be resting times and times when it appeared I was off track in my life. The cards were about me." He took the stack of cards and wrote "A+" on the top one. "You passed the class, Cathy. Looking through all of your important things from the past was part of it. Making the commitment to Spirit to create and see your life as both the in and out breath was the last part. You have graduated."

We all went out and there was a big party going on. Everyone was in exotic costumes. I found a huge gold crown and put it on. It had two small statues of Kyan Yin on the top. Several other people had crowns on too. We talked about how much fun it was to play with the crowns.

I invite you to consider enrolling in this special night college. The curriculum is exciting and challenging. Don't wait for a big crash in your life to begin on your spiritual path. Say yes to Spirit, yes to understanding your dreams and yes to the in-breaths and out-breaths of your life. It is the heart and soul in the circle of life.

See you in class!

Cathy

Twenty-three

How did you start?

Dear Cathy,

How did you start doing healing and psychic work?

Anna

Anna:

Many of the clairvoyants and healers I know have come into this work because of an illness or injury. Many have had near-death experiences like the one I had, and many have had traumatic childhood experiences. Coming to the brink, in whatever way this occurs, is a way of moving the externalized "stuff," the stuff that fills our daily lives, out of the way. This is a place where no one travels with you. You are alone with your experience in a silent space which allows the voice of Spirit to begin to be heard.

A car crash propelled me into such an experience, an opportunity to embrace personal truths about who I truly am, an opportunity to say yes to intuition and healing. I realize now this experience began long before the car crash.

Part of my story is that my father drank when I was young. My little girl story is very connected to how my life was affected by drinking and family patterns around drinking. My story includes my own drinking as a young adult and still later me as the mother of a teen who had a problem with drinking.

Every life story can be told from several different levels. On the level of "little scared girl," I would tell my "victim" story. The same story spoken from a God-connected place changes complexion completely.

We all make choices about how we view our stories. Each level of the story holds its own truths and all are valid. If I choose to see the world through the eyes of a victim, I can so thoroughly identify with this role that I believe this is my only truth. Each day we can look around at all the hurts and injustices in the world and confirm our personal truth. The world is not a safe place. Through practice we can connect to the God place in our personal stories and shift the perspective to a level where we see what the bigger truth is in our lives.

The little girl inside me tells the story by saying, "My dad was sometimes very angry when he drank. It was scary to be around him." When I can move back into that God place I see the experience from a different perspective. Every time I arrived home and went to open the front door and step into my house, I did not know what to expect; so as a child I learned to read the energy of what was happening in the house. I energetically knew what was happening before I opened that door. I knew if I had to head for my bedroom or if it was safe to go upstairs. I knew how to approach my father based on what I read energetically. Even though I can still feel all my feelings about my life, I can now see what an amazing exercise I was provided.

My intuition guides my life and is how I make my living. I am in choice about how I use my intuitive perspective in my personal life. I can say, "Oh, poor Cathy, child of an alcoholic," or I can say, "Wow, look what else was going on." I can see from this different perspective, this God perspective, how I came into my family in agreement with the other spiritual masters so we could all learn together. When we move into the understanding that All is One the entire world becomes a teaching arena. Parents are their children's first spiritual teachers.

I often think about the first days after my crash, how I prayed for healing in my life. I really thought I was praying for recovery from my injuries, but what Spirit had in mind was so different. Every area of my life was unearthed, examined, and kneaded into clarity. This was not an easy road. After the crash some confusing childhood memories started surfacing. I chose to have a period of time when I had no contact with my family. I prayed for guidance in this but could not move out of the hurt child place I was responding from. At the same time these memories were surfacing I was in a period of accelerated spiritual growth and understanding. Every day I was uncovering deeper levels of who I was and releasing pieces of old hurt and feelings of being a victim that were binding me tightly. Because I was coming from this hurt child place my perspective was skewed, and in this distortion I felt my mother was to blame. God seemed to be missing from this place of healing because I could not find the doorway that would lead me into a higher level of understanding.

During my time of healing I had an older woman come to see me as a client. She physically looked like my mother, just in case I was missing it. She said, "I don't know what to do. My daughter says she doesn't want to see me. She blames her father and me for how her life has turned out." I sat across from this woman who was speaking my mother's words to me. At first I didn't know if I could do the session. I was for that moment caught up in all my own stuff. It was like the adult Cathy had disappeared and the nine-year-old Cathy came and sat in my chair. I knew I had been given a unique opportunity and wanted to participate in it, even if I had no idea what was about to be said. I knew if I could stay out of the way, I would gain insight into myself.

I breathed up into the highest realms of myself and began to speak to this woman, every woman's mother, even to myself as a mother. And I listened. Over the next month or so my mother sat in the chair across from me in the form of various clients, and I began to understand our connection in a new way. All of the things that happen to us, both the things that seem good and things that seem bad, lead us to where we are today. Everything that happens shapes us into what we become.

Again, we are going to imagine a group of spiritual masters all sitting down at some huge pre-lifetime planning council. These masters have all spent many lifetimes together offering each other opportunities to grow and learn more about themselves and their connection to Spirit.

Our bodies are a manifestation of all our emotions and thoughts. In this pre-lifetime agreement we decide what we would like to focus on and create a plan so we can offer each other opportunity. We make agreements about our parents and children, and a big picture of the circumstances and opportunities we will have in our life. From this pre-life planning position we see each other clearly and in profound love. Then we move into this life and forget our connections. We forget our connections because when we enter into this teaching field of planet Earth our learning is based on the relationship between our emotions and our creations. If we came in remembering our connections and could perceive each other from that higher level, we would distance ourselves from the experience. All of our experience is not pre-chosen. While we have a general plan of our learning, our day-to-day existence is filled with free choice.

Stop and think about this for a minute. Here we are spiritual masters creating an environment where we can come in and learn huge amounts of information within a very short period of time. We have created an opportunity to remember we create our reality and the key to unlocking manifestation is buried within our own bodies. We have created a playing field offering diversity in our experience and there are a myriad of choices. None are incorrect.

As we go about our daily lives it is easy to get caught up in all the details, seeing what is wrong with everything. I call this the "nose hair level." At the level of looking at someone's nose hairs all we see is what is wrong. When we move up and into our mastery level, understanding the same situation becomes quite different. At the "nose hair level" we make judgments about others' behavior. The way we believe is right and what others believe is wrong. In reality, there is no right or wrong. There is just us, creating opportunities to understand ourselves and our connection to Spirit. From our highest self, we can see who we are, not our behaviors.

On one level we can look back on our life and see the pain caused by our traumas, then based on our perception of the events, live by that perception. Staying at this level of perception, blaming others and holding on to shame, can poison our life. This place of blame and shame uses up so much energy the ability to create in our lives is lost. As we stay in this cycle we weaken our ability to create change in our life.

We have a different choice. We can step back from the situation and see events differently and move into freedom. To do this we must separate from the "little self" and move into that aspect of ourselves that is our God self. Moving perception into this position offers an opportunity to look past the behaviors in each person we encounter.

For me in my life there is no doubt, I am having a human experience. The practice of holding this space of compassion, this master level understanding, gets easier because I do just that, practice. I know, and I know that I know, that at the most connected level All is One. I am so thankful for the grace that led me back to my first spiritual teachers, my family.

Peace to you,

Cathy

Twenty-four

Is it magic?

Dear Cathy,

How do you get things to happen the way you want? Is it magic?

Anna

Anna:

No magic, unless you consider the whole universe magic, and I guess it is! Here is an example of what I think you are asking about.

On a recent trip down to California I arrived at the San Francisco airport late and had missed my small commuter plane connection. I was told that because of overbooking it was highly unlikely a stand-by seat into the small airport I was flying to would be available that day. They issued me a ticket flying to another location back up the coast and then on from there to my final destination. This would have delayed my arrival until late in the evening. After being on a plane since 6 a.m., additional flying up and down the coast several times was not high on my list of fun ways to spend the rest of my day.

I asked the ticket agent to put me on standby anyway, just in case I could get on the plane. I went to work immediately.

- I sat facing the doorway that would lead me out to board the plane.
- I centered myself.
- I imagined a cord going down from the base of my spine to the center of the Earth anchoring me.
- I imagined the top of my head open and energy from Spirit flowing through me.

- I began my prayer: "I know there is one divine force at work in the universe." I waited until that truth resonated through me, then continued. "I am part of that force, part of Spirit manifesting in this body and this experience. I align myself with that truth and feel it deep inside. I am grateful for boarding the next commuter plane and arriving at my destination."

- I felt what it was like to hear my name being called to board the plane.

- I felt myself pick up my bags and hurry up to the line.

- I heard the ticket agent say, "You got on the plane!"

- I imagined the wind hit my face as I walked across the tarmac to board and climbed the steps up into the small plane.

- I imagined sitting down and fastening my seatbelt.

- Imagined the takeoff, the flight and the landing.

- I imagined my friends greeting me at my destination and what it would feel like to receive their hugs.

- I moved into this experience until it was so real I could smell the smells and be totally in the experience.

- Now from the place of all of this, I give thanks for this experience and released it as in completion and done.

- I repeated this process until the moment the plane was boarding.

My name was called!!! I stood up and grabbed my bags just as I had envisioned. The ticket agent said, "I don't know how this happened, but you are on this flight."

Knowing there is one force in the universe, connecting to that force, stating my positive affirmation, giving thanks and letting go. Five easy steps of what is called "Spiritual Mind Treatment." I learned this kind of affirmative prayer through my spiritual community. I would recommend *Living the Science of Mind,* by Ernest Holmes, as a good starting point. Or you might try connecting with the United Centers for Spiritual Living. Many of these communities have teen and young adult programs.

In grace and ease,

Cathy

Twenty-five

How I meditate

Anna:

I meditate every day. This is part of my spiritual practice. Here is my meditation practice. I also have this on a CD if you want to just listen to it.

- Close your eyes and begin breathing slowly and quietly.

- Imagine at the base of your spine there is a cord extending down to the very center of the earth.

- Imagine you can make the cord anything you want. Try making it a beam of light or a waterfall or a chain or a slinky. Notice how different all the different types of cords feel. Just keep it now in the form that works for you.

- Imagine you can make the cord bigger or smaller. Make it as big as the chair you are sitting on; now as big as the room and beyond.

- Bring it in now, making it as thin as a spaghetti noodle. Now try as thin as dental floss. Make the cord exactly the size you like. The size that makes you feel connected to the planet.

- Anchor that cord firmly to the center of the earth.

- Now imagine you can create an opening on the top of your head. Pretend there is a flower with many petals on top of your head, with all the petals pointing up to the sky. Allow the flower to slowly open and as it opens warmth begins to touch your head. Imagine all the energy of Spirit flowing down through the top of your head. Tickly, warm bubbly energy flows down into your neck and shoulders and throughout your body. There is an unlimited source of this energy. Whatever the amount you feel coming in right now, double it.

- Opening now to this Spiritual flow, allow it to wash through you, taking with it all of the thoughts or feelings that no longer serve you. Allow the cord at the base of your spine to act as a drain. Let anything you want to release wash down through your body and out the cord. Release old feelings of anger and rage, grief and sorrow and things from the past you are still holding on to. Release anyone or any event that holds a space in you from wrongs that were done or things you feel sorry about. Just let them go.

- Keep the energy coming in through your head and the connection at the base of your spine.

- Imagine that the arches of your feet can open like the lens of a camera. Get the feeling of opening those points all the way. Pretend that your feet can yawn. Let the energy from the earth itself move up into your legs. Deep, rich forests, the feeling of the shore line, mountains all enter you. Feel that old connection with the planet and let the planet speak to you. Allow yourself to receive steadiness and strength from the planet. When you feel the connection send a message of healing and love back to the planet.

From this relaxed state you can simply think love, or healing, or how you are going to ace the chemistry quiz. Whatever you want to focus on.

Stay in that connected space for as long as you like. You can set a timer so you know when to end or listen to some relaxing music that keeps you centered.

As I end the meditation I repeat the steps that led me into the relaxed state--connection to the earth, to the spiritual realm and to my breath.

The way you sit, hold your hands, cross your legs or have your feet on the floor will all affect how energy runs in your body. Try out different positions and see what you like.

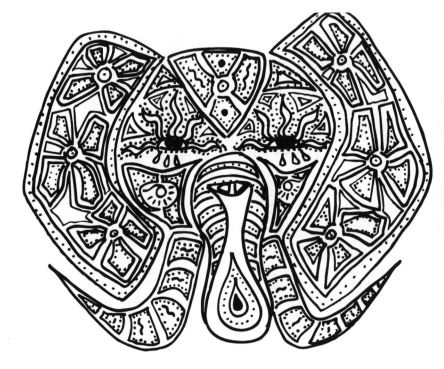

Twenty-six

For sure it gets better

Dear Anna:

Thank you for all the wonderful, thought-provoking questions. Remember these are my ideas. Take what you like, what resonates with you, and leave the rest!

I know you have a lot of questions about the world and how things appear. I have endeavored to answer all your questions to the best of my ability. The thing I really want to let you know is it does get better. It gets better as you grow and find like-minded people to become your peers. It gets better as you learn how to trust your intuition and follow your heart. It gets better as you practice creating your reality and how creating your reality affects everyone around you and even the world.

In the meantime here is a bit of advice:

Take time every day to clear your head. Turn off the TV and computer and just chill. Take a nap, take a walk, draw a picture or just watch the trees. Allow a space for your own still small voice to immerge. This inner guidance system will always lead you well. Sometimes I actually feel pain in my heart if I haven't followed my inner guidance. Let your heart be your guide.

Speak your truth. This does not mean you have to blurt out everything, especially if you have an intuition about some stranger in line at the store. So don't yell out, "Hey, you're going to have a heart attack!" If something like this happens take a deep breath, feel your connection to the planet and know that love surrounds that person. (Taking a deep breath, feeling connection, and knowing there is only love works for every difficult situation!)

You will, without exception, create your own curriculum for what you will need in life. Everything you learn in school is valuable even if it doesn't make sense now. PLUS you will always be creating opportunities for learning through life experiences. Think of it as playing a game like *World of Warcraft* where you are picking up things that appear random until you realize later in the game that you need that special what-not to get past the large hairy beast.

Really, really, really, every new group of enlightened beings see the world they enter as screwed up and on the brink of disaster. You will have your turn to create on this amazing planet. I know it looks like the end of the world but we are simply changing the rules, and the old paradigm no longer works. You are seeing the death of the old way of thinking. The trick is to think outside the box, and that is why you are here.

Okay, this one is really lame. Please wait to have sex. You are a powerful creator. Sex is so much more than feeling good, and it is wonderful. Sex is a HUGE energy exchange. Don't give your power away too easily.

As you grow and evolve you will seek out initiatory experiences. Don't settle for a tattoo of a dolphin or a nose ring. Initiations always have some level of danger and usually mark you permanently from the initiation as an outward sign of your growth. Unlike a piercing that both hurts and marks you, a real initiation is guided by honored elders who have walked your path. The outer marks in a real initiation represent a deep spiritual inner shift.

Just because you are sensitive, creative, intuitive and powerful you don't have to dress the part. Going all Gothic, sullen, and crazy, or being a loner does not improve your overall earth experience. Just be yourself totally. Tell the truth, be kind, and be respectful to all people, animals and the planet. Dressing a certain way doesn't make it so, shining from within does!

Choose your spiritual teachers wisely. Real teachers match all the way through who they are on a spiritual level. If something seems out of whack, they are not the teacher for you. Don't blow off a spiritual teacher because they are old. Rabbis, ministers and teachers all went into that kind of work because it was an expression of who they are spiritually. They might not have all the information you need but they will be a good start. Listen for the parts of their teachings that you resonate with, and remember you don't have to sign up for the whole package of how they see the world. Always be on the lookout for teachers in unexpected places. They might be on your path only a short time so keep your heart open for the truth.

Which leads me to the most important thing I can tell you--always trust your intuition. If you have a feeling about someone it probably is so. Sometimes a first step is revealed that doesn't include the secret of why this step is necessary or what will come next. Trust the process and know that even when it seems like you are in uncharted waters YOU ARE ALWAYS ON TRACK!

So whatever people think you are: a sensitive, psychic, intuitive, a healer or a star child; indigo, crystalline or whatever color radiates from you, who you really are, is you! Right and perfect, here at the right place and right moment, no mistakes, you are Divine! And really, as you grow and find those who resonate with you, for sure it just gets better and better.

You are my apprentice and I am yours.

In grace and ease,
Cathy

About the Author

I was born and raised in the Pacific Northwest.

I have a deep love of ritual and art as spiritual inspiration that was influenced by my experiences being raised Catholic. Some children collected baseball cards; I collected holy cards.

The women in my family have a long history of knowing. When someone was ill or in trouble, and in an age before "caller ID," they would know who was calling on the phone before answering, or they would call a friend or relative to find out what was wrong. This ability was simply explained to me as "the women's thing." This way of being has always been part of my life.

My most important job has been raising my family. Many of my other jobs were extensions of what I was doing as a parent. I have been a childbirth educator, La Leache League leader and dula. I worked at the children's Waldorf School, then taught preschool, then Kindergarten at two different Waldorf Schools. I have been a 4-H leader, active in the PTA and in the teen camps for United Church of Religious Science, now known as Centers for Spiritual Living.

I had a spiritual awakening in 1988. My life became focused on one idea; that I could experience a level of connectedness to Source; in my body, in this time, right now, whatever the circumstances may appear.

I am into continually expanding my understanding of what it means to be that Presence. It has led me through the healing arts and intuitive arts, into mystery school, and now I am simply into living the mystery.

Our daughters and their families live within 10 minutes of our house, and we have the joy of being integral in our grandchildren's lives. I am surrounded by shiny children all the time.

I am a spiritual coach and metaphysical teacher. I come from a place of knowing that people are already perfect and my job is to help them reveal that perfection.

I am a Science of Mind Practitioner at Genesis Global Spiritual Center in Burien, Washington and I am always a student. I am currently in Ministerial School through the Holmes Institute of Consciousness Studies.

Throughout my life I have found healing in many unexpected ways and I continue to grow and explore my relationship to the Presence that I know we all are.

In grace and ease,
Cathy

Where is Anna today?

First let me say that Anna is very real, and Anna is indeed her name. I had initially changed it, but when I told her the book would be called "Letters to Laura," she did not see herself portrayed as a Laura, so there you go.

Anna is a fantastic, bright and beautiful young woman. She is still in college, and knowing her insatiable curiosity, she will be in school a good long time, ending up with many initials after her name.

She spends as much time as possible studying in Europe, and is always surprised and delighted when she receives grants and is admitted to special programs. Who wouldn't want her in their program?

Anna plans on being a college professor and speaks several languages including Yiddish.

I could point to her parents and the many supportive adults in Anna's life and credit them for the amazing way she has turned out. The real credit goes of course to Anna herself; bright, shiny, multi-colored-aura Anna. She told me she has many more questions for me.

About the illustrations

All the illustrations in this book are original drawings by Cathy Pfeil and are available as posters and cards.

PAGE	TITLE	MEDIA
6	Look for the Ox	Sumi-e ink and brush
8	Flowers	Pen
16	Catching a Glimpse of the Ox	Sumi-e ink and brush
24	Rooted Snow Leopard	Sumi-e ink and brush
36	Ox in Full View	Sumi-e ink and brush
40	Fish and Dragonfly	Pen
54	Taming the Ox	Sumi-e ink and brush
62	Riding Home	Crayon
66	Touch Drawing	ink mono-print with R&L hands
78	Riding Home	Sumi-e ink and brush
94	Epoch Archetypes	Pen
98	Returning to Gaia	Sumi-e ink and brush
108	Ox in Full View	Crayon
124	Elephant	Pen
132	Returning to the Marketplace	Sumi-e ink and brush
134	Endozo	Sumi-e ink and Brush